HAS GOD INDEED SAID?

WILLIAMS OSSAI

HAS

GOD

INDEED SAID?

WILLIAMS OSSAI

Has God Indeed Said?

Copyright © 2022

Has God Indeed Said?

Qualified Rights Reserved.
No part of this book may be transmitted, reproduced or distributed by any electronic or mechanical means. And no part of it may be altered, plagiarized or otherwise used for any other commercial purposes without permission from the publisher.

Layout, Cover Design and Publishing by
Merite Book Hub
United Kingdom
Whatsapp: +234 (0) 8164803146
+44785315561

Contact the Author:
Williams Ossai
+234 803 414 9045

DEDICATION

This book is dedicated to believers who are fighting the good fight of faith and desire to live triumphantly above the limitations, struggles, frustrations, and defeats that are in this world.

TABLE OF CONTENTS

TITLE PAGE..I
COPYRIGHT...II
DEDICATION...III
CHAPTER ONE
    THE TWIST...1
CHAPTER TWO
    SEEK TO UNDERSTAND....................................12
CHAPTER THREE
    FIGHT THE GOOD FIGHT 20
CHAPTER FOUR
    ANOTHER GOSPEL...33
CHAPTER FIVE
    EVIL AWARENESS..49
CHAPTER SIX
    THE KINGDOM FIRST...58
CHAPTER SEVEN
    ABOUT GIVING, PRAYER, AND FASTING............75

Has God Indeed Said?

This is all that I have learned: God made us plain and simple, but we have made ourselves very complicated.
Ecclesiastes 7:29 GNT

INTRODUCTION

The word of God for fruitfulness in life is usually very simple and not complex or tedious. The enemy, knowing that the word of God, just like a seed, has the capacity to yield a full harvest of what it talks about, will slither in to question what God has said, plants doubt, and makes it seem impossible for the word to be obeyed.

This technique of the devil is almost as old as time itself and we must see to it that we do not fall into this trap by making fellowship with the word and the Holy Spirit a daily priority. Devote yourself to the study of the Word and the Holy Spirit will reveal to you all that has been given to you in Christ for a life of unending success.

Now the serpent was more cunning than any beast of the field which the Lord God had made. And he said to the woman, **"Has God indeed said,** *'You shall not eat of every tree of the garden'?" Genesis 3:1.*

Sometimes we may hear a voice distorting the Logos (the written Word of God) in an attempt to mislead. The distorted version may actually resemble the word of God and without the guidance and counsel of the Holy Spirit, may be accepted and acted upon as truth.

God's word/instruction is His answer to every situation/circumstance in life and comes with the grace for total obedience. However, the enemy picks up the word, twists it, and presents to you a totally misleading yet beguiling version meant to bring about your disobedience and downfall.

Has God Indeed Said?

For our love for God means that we obey his commands. And his commands are not too hard for us, because every child of God is able to defeat the world. And we win the victory over the world by means of our faith. 1 John 5:3-4 GNT.

CHAPTER 1
THE TWIST

The tree of life was also in the midst of the garden, and the tree of the knowledge of good and evil.
(Genesis 2:9 NKJV)

In the beginning, God prepared the Garden of Eden and garnished it with every beautiful and good thing for Adam and Eve to enjoy. Amongst all the wonderful features of the garden, was the tree of life, which was in the center of the garden, as well as the tree of the knowledge of good and evil. (Genesis 2:9).

Everything was theirs to explore and enjoy. The only proviso was that they were not to eat of the tree of the knowledge of good and evil. A contravention of this would have dire consequences. Life in Eden was not one of assumption. Adam and Eve had received specific terms and conditions from God, for their life and residency in Eden.

And the Lord God commanded the man, saying, **"Of every tree of the garden you may freely eat;** *but of the tree of the knowledge of good and evil you shall not eat, for in the day that you eat of it* **you shall surely die."** *Genesis 2:16-17.*

We see from the above text that God's instruction gave them liberty to enjoy His blessings fully and freely, within lovingly placed boundaries. The death sentence for non-compliance, was not ambiguous but also clearly enunciated by God.
When the voice of contradiction and deception came from the serpent, dripping with deceptive interest and concern, it asked: *"Has God indeed said,* **'you shall not eat of every tree** *of the garden'?" Genesis 3:1.*

It is important to reiterate here that what God said is,

"Of every tree of the garden you may freely eat, but of the tree of the knowledge of good and evil you shall not eat." Genesis 2:16.

The serpent's cunning and subtle misrepresentation, categorized every tree in the garden, including the tree of life as forbidden, whilst promoting as advantageous, the very tree forbidden by God. This is in direct contradiction to God's intentions and instructions. The devil's insinuations presented bondage (starvation) and death.

Sadly, the damage was done. The devil succeeded in planting sufficient doubt in Eve's heart during the conversation to cause her to carefully consider the forbidden tree and seducing her to transgression in her words and actions.

And when the woman saw that the tree was good for food, and that it was pleasant to the eyes; and a tree to be desired to make one wise; she took of the fruit thereof, and did eat; and gave also to her husband with her, and he did eat. Genesis 3:16.

Suddenly, the woman could discern absolutely nothing in the fruit of the tree which showed it to be bad, harmful, or unfit to be eaten. As far as the optical eyes could see, it showed great promise of being delicious, nutritious, and nourishing, contradicting God's verdict. Also, the tree excelled all the other trees because it was to be desired to make one wise as the serpent implied. So why did God forbid it as food? Eve may have rationalized.

It is important to observe that Eve at the onset, did not just crumble like a pack of cards when the serpent engaged her. She put up some form of defense which showed that she had indeed received information (God's instruction) regarding the tree of the knowledge of good and evil. Regrettably it was not full, sufficient, or adequate to neutralize the adversary, neither did she know how to effectively act on the information she had received.

And the woman said to the serpent, "We may eat the fruit of the trees of the garden; but of the fruit of the tree which is in the midst of the garden, God has said, 'You

*shall not eat it, **nor shall you touch it**, lest you die.'"*
Genesis 3:2-3.

Notice that nowhere in God's instruction did He say Adam and Eve should not touch the fruit of the tree, even though it was advisable to steer away from the tree completely. Due to Eve's scant understanding or lack of familiarity with God's Word, she expanded God's instruction from "Eat Not" to also "Touch Not." Suddenly God's commands took up new proportions; beyond what it demanded. The presence of the tree of the knowledge of good and evil in the garden was suddenly gaining more attention and significance than necessary. Touching the tree had now become disobedience for Eve. The simple instruction had, thanks to the enemy, become complex and tiresome. The result? Disobedience.

*For I am jealous for you with godly jealousy. For I have betrothed you to one husband, that I may present you as a chaste virgin to Christ. But I fear, lest somehow, as the serpent deceived Eve by his craftiness, so your minds may be corrupted from the **simplicity that is in Christ**. For if he who comes preaches **another Jesus*** *whom we have not preached, or if you receive **a different spirit** which you have not received, or **a different gospel** which you have not accepted — you may well put up with it! 2 Corinthians 11:2-4.*

Also, from the entire dialogue between Eve and the serpent in Genesis 3, it can be deduced that Eve was in proximity to the forbidden tree. The bible records that after she had carefully considered the tree, she *"took of its fruit and ate."* She did not have to go to the tree again, possibly she simply reached out and took the fruit. Adam and Eve received a command not to eat the **fruit**, it would have also been wise to avoid being near the **tree**.

*Do not enter **the path** of the wicked, and do not walk in **the way** of evil. Avoid it, do not travel on it; turn away from it and pass on. Proverbs 4:1415.*

One can avoid evil by staying away from **the way** of it. Their closeness to the tree could make it even more appealing and subject for discussion. Likewise, there are many who have been drawn into destructive vices and habits due to their being around the activities that lead to them.

The bible admonishes us to *"abstain from all appearance of evil"* 1 Thessalonians 5:22; if it appears evil, stay away from it. And bible also instructs in 1 Peter 2:1 *(the message translation)*, *"exercise your freedom by serving God, not by breaking the rules"*; do not allow your freedom to lead you into sin.

Even the Lord Jesus was not spared by Satan's attempts to cause the Master to call in question the declaration of His divine Sonship (Matthew 3:17). The deceiver confronted Jesus directly and taking advantage of His present circumstances; twisted and contradicted God's Word seeking to trap the Master into sin (Matthew 4:3): *"If you are the son of God, command that these stones become bread."* The word "If" in the statement, questions the Lord's Sonship. How did the Lord Jesus respond? By ignoring the devil hoping he would go away, fretting over His present circumstances of hunger and weakness, and wondering why angels had not brought Him sustenance? Absolutely not!

The bible confirms how Jesus responded: *"But He answered and said, it is written, 'Man shall not live by bread alone, but by every word that proceeds from the mouth of God.'* Matthew 4:4.

Jesus' response was voiced out in line with the written word of God. His response centered on God's Word, not His circumstances, and was spoken from a position of knowledge, faith, and authority. This is how to act on God's Word. The Master has left us an example worthy of emulation and guaranteed to work. Refuse to voice out fear or doubt but always voice your faith in God's Word.

*This book of the law shall not depart out of thy **mouth**; but thou shalt **meditate** therein day and night, that thou mayest **observe to do** all that is written therein: for then thou shalt make thy way prosperous, and then thou shalt have good success. Joshua 1:8.*

A well-known and very often quoted scripture but not so often acted upon, especially in the face of challenges. In the text above, it is important to observe that the emphasis is the Word being always in the mouth and not only staying in the heart. In other words, we must continually speak God's Word or speak in consistence with God's word. I want to draw your attention to this simple truth as we can see that it is not only the amount of the Word of God you think you know that makes you succeed in life, but the Word of God you speak, meditate, and live in consistent with that gives you victory in life.

The scripture enjoins that the Word of God dwell in us richly in all wisdom (Colossians 3:16). Our understanding and precise application of God's word is key to maintaining our victory in life and not fall prey to Satan and his cohorts of darkness.

THE SIMPLE INSTRUCTION: Come
So He said, "Come." And when Peter had come down out of the boat, he walked on the water to go to Jesus. Matthew 14:29.

Just a four-letter command, COME; reassuring in its simplicity and efficacy to keep Peter ON THE WATER. Peter had the "ON THE WATER" experience as he took those few (literal) steps towards Jesus in obedience and faith. Alas when Peter saw the boisterous wind, he was afraid; and beginning to sink, he cried out, "Lord, save me!"

And Jesus **immediately** stretched out His hand and caught him, and said to him, "O you of little faith, why did you doubt?" (Matthew 14:25-31).

One could reason, in Peter's defense, that if the wind had not become boisterous, Peter would have maintained his balance on the water and walk undisturbed. Maybe so but note that the same boisterous wind did not adversely affect Jesus, who was still ON the water at the same time Peter was sinking.

For the little distance in which Peter demonstrated his faith in Christ, he was upheld by His power. His faith in Jesus suspended the natural laws of gravity on Peter. But when his fear overpowered his faith, the natural laws reverted to their predetermined action, thereby he began to sink.

What do you see?
The issue with Peter's sinking was not the violent wind, but that he contemplated or regarded the wind.

Note that Peter became afraid and started sinking right before Jesus, so he did not sink due to the absence of Jesus, but due to doubt and fear as he looked AWAY from Jesus and SAW the boisterous wind.

In the challenges and circumstances of life, it matters what you see, or rather what you train yourself to see.

If you look at the boisterous winds of the challenges or difficulties with optical eyes, you will drown. Instead keep your gaze fixed on God's Word with the eyes of faith. Refuse to SEE the doctor's report or the symptoms of unwellness in your body. Refuse to see that your account is in the red. Refuse to see the challenges in your home or marriage. Refuse to see that hopeless situation. Refusing to see does not mean denying the facts but refusing the situation or challenge to have any power over you.

Remember, Eve **saw** that the tree was good for food and pleasant to the eyes. Based on what she saw, she transgressed.

Hold on to God's command. No matter what life throws at you, refuse to give in or give up. If Adam and Eve had remained totally submitted to God's authority in the garden without subscribing to the serpent's opinion, they would have continued to enjoy life eternally. Remember the tree of life was not prohibited. They were free to eat as much as they wanted from it.

Dear friend, it is time to see differently if you want to get the results that are consistent with God's Word.

And the Lord said to Abram, after Lot had separated from him: "**Lift your eyes now and look from the place where you are** — *northward, southward, eastward, and westward; for all the land which you see I give to you and your descendants forever. Genesis 13:14-15.*

Let us take a close look at the emphasized portion of the above text. At the time of this command, Abram had not yet become Abraham. He had unfulfilled desires. His life was full of questions: why? How? and when?

- *Lift your eyes:* Take your gaze away from the challenges, the unfulfilled desires, the needs, difficulties, pain, and the unpleasant conditions.
- *"NOW"*: not later! Not when things start getting better. Not when you get the job. Not when you get pregnant. Not when you are married. Not when you become wealthy. Not when you feel comfortable. Not when you have time. No!
  God says lift your eyes NOW.
- *Look from the place where you are*: Not look at the place where you are. Do not look at the situations or conditions but LOOK FROM IT! It does not matter how hopeless the case may be. Look from that peculiar, specific place and fix your gaze on God's Word concerning that situation.
- Indeed, what you see is what you get: *"for all the land which you see I give to you and your descendants forever."*

A sure promise of tangible asset (land – territory) would be brought forth by Abram following God's command. He left his fatherland to follow the Lord holding unto His word as assurance of inheritance for himself and his descendants. Incredible.

The two of the most employed fiery darts of the wicked one against our faith in God are fear and doubt. The only prescribed antidote to fear and doubt is the Word of God. How much of it do you have? Are you skilled in handling the Word of truth? No matter the challenges of life, it's important what you pay attention to. Give attention to the Word of God and hold firm notwithstanding the boisterous winds (situations and circumstances). Reject the beguiling voice that tempt you to look away from the Lord.

And when they got into the boat, the wind ceased. Matthew 14:32. Child of God! Did you hear that? **The wind ceased!**

Get into the same boat with the Lord. That life-threatening, painful, embarrassing, and distressing situation is guaranteed to cease if you stick with the Word and maintain your confession of God's Word.

In 2 Corinthians 4:17, we are assured that our light affliction is but for a moment. In other words, it has a termination point, and light (not heavy as it seems).

While we look not at the things which are seen, but at the things which are unseen: for the things which are seen are temporal; but the things which are not seen are eternal. 2 Corinthians 4:18.

CHAPTER 2

SEEK TO UNDERSTAND

These (the Berean Jews) were more noble than those in Thessalonica, in that they received the word with all readiness of mind, and searched the scriptures daily, whether those things were so (Acts 17:11 KJV)

Dear friend, in the previous chapter, we established that to win in life, regardless of the circumstances, a full knowledge and precise application of God's Word is key. This will ensure that, for you, the victorious life is not an event but a **lifestyle**.

God's glory in your life is directly proportional to the revelation of God's Word in your spirit. The Word of God is God's vision, opinion, thought, law and principle for life and success. To put it succinctly, the Word of God is your life.

*For it (the Word) is not a vain thing for you; because **it is your life**: and through this thing ye shall prolong your days in the land, whither ye go over to Jordan to possess it. Deuteronomy 32:47.*

The above scripture emphasizes the significance and value of the Word of God in our lives. Dear Child of God, it is important to note here that **there is a method to God's Word**. It is not enough to just think you know the Word. How you interact with and apply the word is important if you must get the desired results.

Take for instance, someone is given a doctor's prescription to treat a particular ailment. The prescription will always come with the recommended dosage, timing and how the medication should be taken (with food, before or after a meal, etc.) Failure to adhere strictly with these instructions will not effectively treat the ailment nor yield the expected results. In many instances, disregarding medical prescriptions may give rise to health complications.

The opening text highlights the attitude, disposition, and manners of the Berean Jews regarding God's Word. They were eager and enthusiastic to hear, and willing and ready to believe and accept. **They took the time <u>daily</u>** to diligently study and examine, meditate upon, and acquaint themselves intimately with the Word. They received the Word not merely notionally but spiritually and experimentally.

Note that these Jews searched the scriptures **daily** whether those things they heard were so. They did not doubt the apostles' message, but they wanted to confirm for themselves that the things the apostles preached concerning the Messiah: His incarnation, sufferings, death, and resurrection from the dead, corresponded with the writings of the OLD Testament.

Of course, they confirmed the apostles' message as absolute truth, embraced the teachings fully and lived accordingly (Acts 17:12). The Jews in

Thessalonica, on the other hand, as the scripture tells us, also heard the same Gospel, but sadly they had the wrong disposition and attitude towards the message. They were bigoted, opinionated and prejudiced against the Word of God so they did not believe the Word nor obey it.

Acts 17:2 says that Paul reasoned with them (the Thessalonian Jews) out of the scriptures. He used analytical and logical arguments they could not disprove. They did not readily receive the message which necessitated his preaching to them for three Sabbaths. The result? Some of the Jews believed but not a great number, because of their prejudice against Christ and His Gospel (Acts 17:4-9).

What is your attitude and disposition regarding the Word of God? Like the Berean Jews, are you excited to hear the Word? Do you give attention and priority to the scriptures? Do you create the time **daily** to study God's word? Are you growing in grace and in the knowledge of God's Word? Is the Word of God working in your life?

If your answer to all these soul-searching questions is not a resounding YES, then there may be a challenge with the amount of God's Word in you or lack of skill in applying the Word to your life.

Hosea 4:6 says "my *people are destroyed for lack of knowledge.*" Lack here means either a total absence or inadequate and insufficient knowledge. Either of the two scenarios bode destruction and calamity.

Lack of knowledge is ignorance: unfamiliarity, unawareness, and inexperience. Does this describe you in relation to God's Word? If it does, it doesn't matter how many degrees and qualifications you have, your proficiency in business, your birth and pedigree, your connections and associations, life will be a struggle.

Indeed, many of God's people are living not only ungodly lives but lack-luster, tasteless, unfruitful, and unsuccessful lives simply because they lack the knowledge of God and His Word.

The devil's strategy is to eradicate or drastically decrease the Word level in your life. He wants to keep you ignorant, uninformed, unskilled, and unresponsive. That way, you cannot live a glorious, happy life.

For unto us was the gospel preached, as well as unto them: but the Word preached did not profit them, not being mixed with faith in them that heard it. Hebrews 4:2.

From the above text, we see that the Word of God is preached to us that we may profit by it. Unfortunately, there are many unprofitable hearers today who gain nothing. It is a sorry state indeed for anyone who hears the Word but does not profit from it or is not blessed by it. It still points to the how (the manner and the attitude) with which we receive the Word. Do you believe the Word, accept it and in faith act on it (apply it to your life) or are you cynical, doubtful, disbelieving, and full of fear?

The bible tells us with the heart man believes (Romans 10:10). Believing the Gospel is not just an intellectual exercise. You receive the word with your mind and believe in your heart. You must make up your mind and open your heart!

Overcoming temptation

Once Jesus was supernaturally identified as beloved Son of God during His water baptism (Matthew 3:16-17), one would think that that was sufficient grounds to launch out immediately into full and public ministry. On the contrary, no one could find Him for He went into seclusion in the wilderness of Judea for forty days and forty nights.

It was there that Jesus encountered Satan (a Hebrew word meaning the 'accuser') and was thrice tempted. 'Satan' (or the 'devil') is the one who accuses people at the final judgement, and who tempts people to follow man's ways instead of God's ways (see Job 1:1-12, Zechariah 3:1-2, 1 Chronicles 21:1).

In Jesus' first temptation, the devil took advantage of the master's hunger and commanded that He turn stones to bread (Matthew 4:3). Now the Judaean Desert is a barren, rocky desert. Some stones are coated in soft lime and curiously resemble loaves of bread – increasing the potency of the temptation. Although Jesus had the power to turn stones into bread, He resisted Satan's suggestion by quoting from the Jewish scriptures: *"A person does not live by eating only bread, but by everything God says"* (Matthew 4:4, Deuteronomy 8:3).

The 3 major temptations that Jesus encountered in the wilderness, were all overcome with the word of God. At each instance, Jesus declared or spoke the scripture **once** to liquidate the temptation. Pause for a moment, and consider how it was possible for Jesus to defeat the devil with just one scripture each time?

Question. Why did Eve not get the same results Jesus did? She also responded to the devil, quoting God's Word on the matter.
In the preceding chapter, we established that there was a discrepancy in her response with what God said. She did not have a full understanding of the instruction and therefore could not successfully thwart the devil.

Study *to shew thyself approved unto God, a workman that needeth not to be ashamed,* **rightly dividing the Word of truth.** *2 Timothy 2:15.*

Child of God, there is a technique to the Word of God. Responding to challenges or adversity is not just about quoting scriptures, it is about speaking with deep rooted conviction in line with what God has said concerning you.

So that we may boldly say, the Lord is my helper, and I will not fear what man shall do to me. Hebrews 13:6

The words *"so that"* indicate that verse 6 is a continuation of what was being said in verse 5. The fifth verse says, *"for He hath said, I will never leave thee, nor forsake thee"*. The sixth verse was not a quote or verbatim of the declaration in the fifth, but it was what the writer received in faith, personalized, and declared based on his full understanding and faith in what the scripture said.

So daily you should make such declarations, "The glory of God is evident in my health, finances, family, business, and ministry. I am unstoppable. I must be whom God has made me to be. Christ in me is my guarantee of perfect health, prosperity, and success". Amen! Your faith filled declarations will keep you in perpetual victory over Satan's schemes and stratagems.

The interplay of the seed and the soil
The parable of the Sower is another illustration of how the enemy attacks the Word you receive. In all the four illustrations, all the seeds were sown. It wasn't the seed nor the sowing that determined the harvest, but the ground that received the seed determined the fruitage.

The seeds that fell on the wayside are those who heard the Word but did not understand it, and the devil came to steal the word from them (Matthew 13:18-19). Lack of understanding opens invitation to the devil.

The seeds that fell on the rock described those who heard the Word of God and received it with joy, but the Word had no root (Luke 8:13). This set of people have the Word, but the Word does not save them from temptation or crises. This is because there is no depth to the knowledge of the Word of God they possess. Remember the scripture admonishes that the Word should dwell in you richly in all wisdom (Colossians 3:16). The word "richly" implies abundance and copiousness as opposed to scarcity and deficiency. So, with the Word of God, quantity and quality matter.

Study to shew thyself approved unto God, a workman that needeth not to be ashamed, **rightly dividing the word of truth.** *2 Timothy 2:15.*

The amplified version explains the highlighted portion better: *correctly analyzing and accurately dividing (rightly handling and skillfully teaching) the Word of God.*

This is what neutralizes the fiery darts of the enemy – rightly handling the Word of God. This skill can only be strengthened and honed by spending time studying the Word and fellowshipping with the Holy Spirit.

Study requires dedication, diligence, much reading, taking notes, analysis, research, application, prayer, and meditation.

The bible declares that the Word of God is the sword of the Spirit. Can you put a sword in the hands of a toddler to ward off intruders? Absolutely not for he would not have the skill to use it.

The word of God always works when used rightly. Build your skill and dexterity in the Word.

Child of God, give attention to God's Word and your life will be increasingly excellent and full of glory.

CHAPTER 3
FIGHT THE GOOD FIGHT

For whatever is born of God overcomes the world. And this is the victory that has overcome the world — our faith. (1 John 5:4) Victory: A successful ending of a struggle or contest.

Overcome: To win a victory over.

The two words, overcome and victory infer a battle or fight. In the Christian faith, we have the **work** of Christianity, the **walk** of Christianity and the **war** of Christianity.

The work of Christianity: Our evangelical efforts and prayers to reach and save the lost e.g., outreach programs etc.

The walk of Christianity: Our everyday activities of our Christian life through which we relate with one another and relate with God e.g., study, meditation, speaking the truth, forgiving, etc.

The war of Christianity: Our onslaught against the forces of darkness that attempt to oppose and frustrate God's agenda and plan, e.g., casting out demons, securing territory (home, local assembly, place or work/assignment, community, etc.), faith declarations, etc.

A lot of Christians are aware of the walk and work of Christianity but may not be cognizant of the war of Christianity. And because of their lack of awareness, they are not primed and prepared for battle, hence suffer defeat in life.

For though we walk (live) in the flesh, we are not carrying on our warfare according to the flesh and using mere human weapons. 2 Corinthians 10:3.

Child of God, life is war. The bible enjoins us to *fight the good fight of faith* (1 Timothy 6:12). You are right in the thick of this battle. You cannot pretend it is not ongoing, neither can you avoid it, nor wish it away. It is a battle over your life, children, marriage, family, ministry, finances, business, career, your environment, nation, and all that pertains to life and godliness.

The battle is tagged a fight of faith not a fight of wit, intellect, or strength. Why is it called a fight of faith? Because faith is the weapon and victory. The fight is important because it helps build us strong and invincible and enables us lay hold of the eternal life that is able to keep us fruitful, productive and successful regardless of the circumstances.

It is a fight to uphold the Word of God, unleash our faith through our faith filled declarations, and see it prevail over every contrary situation or challenge. If we prevail in the fight of faith, we will enjoy a life of perpetual triumph and glory here on earth.

Fight the good fight of faith, lay hold on eternal life, to which you were also called and have confessed the good confession in the presence of many witnesses. 1 Timothy 6:12.

There are those who struggle through life because they are ineffective in the fight of faith. They lack the requisite knowledge, wisdom, and faith.

If thou faint in the day of adversity, thy strength is small. Proverbs 24:10.

Faith is not wishful thinking or having a strong desire. Faith is an action word, action fully backed up by God's word. As you prevail in this fight, you consistently make forward and upward progress in life. Child of God, do not pack your bags in defeat, don't throw in the towel, don't give up. Keep pushing.

You may ask so how exactly do we fight this war?

*This charge I commit unto thee, son Timothy, **according to the prophecies which went before on thee, that*** *thou by them mightiest war a good warfare. 1 Timothy 1:18.*

Prophecy is a strategy of the Spirit. It is a strategy of war. There are Spirit filled words that guide your future as a believer in Christ.

In prophecy, you are declaring words of power over your life inspired by the Holy Spirit. You use those prophecies against challenges of life.

For instance, the first attack Satan launched on Jesus in the wilderness was focused on questioning His Sonship as we mentioned earlier. Satan started with statement *"If you are the son of God…"* Prior to this, Jesus had been declared the Son of God and we saw God spoke from heaven saying, *"This is my beloved son in whom I am well pleased."* Jesus overcame the temptation; He has not forgotten whom He is in God. As a child of God, there are words over your life on whom you are in God. You win battles in life from that place of awareness.

Paul in the above scripture drew Timothy's attention to the words that had been spoken concerning him. Paul went on to say, *"that thou by them."* Paul charged Timothy to use those words (prophecy) to fight a good fight. It wasn't a responsibility that Timothy could delegate to another because Paul emphasized that he was to fight. Also, Paul expected Timothy to be well acquainted with the prophecies, if not, he could not be expected to use them to fight the good fight effectively.

Child of God, what has God said concerning you in the scriptures or during your personal devotion? By those words, make declarations of faith over your life and family. Do not delegate the fight to your leader or pastor or prayer partner. It is your responsibility, so get up and fight. Like Abraham, refuse to consider the adversities. Keep declaring God's Word. You will surely come back with a testimony.

"If you can't fly, run. If you can't run, walk. If you can't walk, crawl.
But by all means keep moving." - Dr. Martin Luther King Jr.

To win in this battle, you require strong faith therefore you need to build your faith strong.

So then faith cometh by hearing, and hearing by the Word of God. Romans 10:17.

Spend time hearing the Word of God consistently and continuously, day and night (Psalm 1). Invest in messages, books and tapes that teach God's Word. Don't speed read the scriptures. It is not a novel, neither is it a sports or fashion magazine. Be intentional about studying and meditating on the scriptures. Your study time should include not only your bible and devotional, but writing materials (notebook and pen), and other bible study aids for enhanced learning. When you show the Holy Spirit that you are eager and ready to learn, He will illuminate your understanding of the person, character and will of the Father as well as reveal to you, who you are and what you have in Christ.

Dear child of God, give the Word of God priority in your daily living. You will end up ineffective, weak, unstable, and unproductive if you allow yourself to be distracted by spending precious time engaging and entertaining yourself on social media, movies or non-value adding activities or hobbies.

The psalmist says, *"I will delight myself in thy statutes: I will not forget thy word". Psalms 119:16.*

This book wouldn't have been a reality if I had given all my time to the pressures of this life. There were so many things clamoring for my time and attention simultaneously. I have a very demanding job from sunup to sundown. In my free time at work, I am on social media to get some relevant information or catch up on events. I realized that I had become a slave to my work instead of writing this book which the Lord instructed I write. I had to discipline myself by isolating myself very early in the morning and ensuring that I focus on the Word during that time without distractions. During my quiet time, the Holy Spirit not only gave me the muchneeded inspiration for the book, but He also gave me time to actually write. To my amazement, I found out that I could write, and my work did not suffer. What changed? I gave God's Word its proper place.

Dear Child of God never let the challenges and circumstances of life take you away from fellowshipping with the Word. Spend time building your faith for your faith is the Victory.

The Mustard Seed
*So Jesus said to them, "Because of your unbelief; for assuredly, I say to you, if you have **faith as a mustard seed**, you will say to this mountain, 'Move from here to there,' and it will move; and nothing will be impossible for you. Matthew 17:20.*

I always used to read this scripture as "if you have faith as **small as** a mustard seed…." until a beloved brother, Bishop Ukaegbu Ogwo, corrected me by pointing out that Jesus never said to have faith as small as a mustard seed but *"as a mustard seed."*

A lot of people have made the same mistake thinking that you need just little faith to move the mountains of life. I had to conscientiously study that scripture in Matthew 17:20, and with the help of the Holy Spirit, I made a great discovery. Yes, the mustard seed is very small, but that same small seed grows into the giant oak tree. When Jesus spoke of your faith being as the mustard seed, He was referring to the growth potential of your faith, like the mustard seed, to become very great. There may be other small or even tiny seeds but unlike the mustard, not many may have the capacity to grow into a giant tree.

Jesus, at another instance, alluded to the growth potential of the mustard seed in Mark 4:31-32. Saying *'it becomes greater than all herbs and shooteth out great branches."* The principal here is on the growth potential and not on the size.

The bible says in Romans 12:3, that God has dealt to every man the measure of faith. As a born-again Christian, you have a certain measure of faith. It is up to you to grow your faith. Exercise your faith muscles by using it. It is okay to start small, but do not remain a babe in faith.

The devil has distorted this same scripture and deceived many to think that they don't need to grow their faith. Afterall with small faith Jesus said you can move mountains. He constantly emphasizes the small size of the mustard seed and blindsides you to the growth potential of the mustard seed.

"He staggered not at the promise of God through unbelief; but was strong in faith, giving glory to God" Romans 4:20

Who is the Opposition?

If the bible talks about a battle, then surely there is an enemy or opposition. Sadly, many spend their time and energy boxing the air, on the wrong target.

Please note that the battle of faith is not a battle against an annoying neighbor, a wicked relative, an uncaring spouse, or a mean employer.

"For we wrestle not against flesh and blood, but against principalities, against powers, against the rulers of the darkness of this world, against spiritual wickedness in high places". Ephesians 6:12.

The devil is the adversary, together with his wicked spirits, devils, and minions. These are all spirits who may attack a believer through a human host (a person), policy, system, or government or a bodily affliction. It is not your place to fight the person, organization, or agency through which they operate thereby distracting yourself. Always recognize the one behind the attack.

1 Peter 5:8 reveals the adversary as the devil so your mother-in-law or uncle or stepmother is not the problem. Don't fight them but always address the spirit behind their actions.

There were many instances in the scriptures where the Lord Jesus looked beyond the person or persons and addressed the devil behind their actions.
1. *"But He turned, and said unto Peter, Get thee behind me Satan:*
    thou art an offence unto me: for thou savourest not the things that be of God, but those that be of men" Matthew 16:23.

2. *When I was daily with you in the temple, ye stretched forth no hands against me: but this is your hour and the power of darkness" Luke 22:53.*

Being Battle Ready

The fight of faith is so called because we are sufficiently equipped for it, and we are guaranteed victory.

It is important to note that since it is not a battle against men, we cannot employ manmade weapons or techniques.

"For the weapons of our warfare are not carnal, but mighty through God to the pulling down of strongholds". 2 Corinthians 10:4

"Not carnal" means not physical (weapons of flesh and blood).

Ephesians 6:12 itemizes all the offensive and defensive weapons in our God given armory as follows:

- Loins girded with truth
- The breastplate of righteousness
- Feet shod with the preparation of the gospel of peace
- The shield of faith

- The helmet of salvation
- The sword of the Spirit which is the Word of God and goes alongside prayer
- Watching
- Praying for one another

"Put on the whole armour of God, that ye may be able to stand against the wiles of the devil". Ephesians 6:11.

Child of God, this is not a suggestion but a command by the one who enlists us in the battle. Be lacking in none. This is not time to cherry pick or to say like David did to Saul: *"I cannot go with these, (Saul's armour, helmet and sword), for I am not used to them. And David took them off "1 Samuel 17:39.*

You cannot afford to take off, discard or do without a single item from the prescribed list. God commands that you, yes you, child of God put on the whole armour. It is your duty. Don't wait to be clothed by God as Saul clothed David for the battle. You require the whole armour to stand against the wiles and stratagems of Satan, to oppose his schemes and machinations and resist his temptations. Remember it is called the armour of God because it is prepared by God Himself for His people and because the efficacy of it is from Him. It is whole, complete, and perfect and all of it is necessary and useful. No part is to be neglected but all to be taken and put on so that no part or area of your life is vulnerable and defenseless.

The armour of God is the proof against all the might and craft of Satan. So, child of God, always remain in battle ready position to repel any new attack.

It is observable that, among all the offensive and defensive battle requirements, there is none for the back. If you turn your back on the enemy, you lie exposed. Stand on your guard always. Never be caught unaware.

"Be sober, be vigilant; because your adversary the devil, as a roaring lion, walketh about, seeking whom he may devour. 1 Peter 5:8

The story is told of a battle between the army of Israel and the Syrian army. The king of Israel thrashed the Syrians. However, a prophet warned the king of Israel after his victory, to fortify himself and be battle ready for the king of Syria, early the following year would attack again (1 Kings 20:1-22).

The adversary will not lick his wounds after a defeat, he will regroup, and attack again so do not be careless. Jesus was tempted by Satan thrice consecutively and thereafter departed from him until an opportune time (Luke 4:13). Always be on your guard. Be vigilant.

God's word is not a suggestion on how to live your life. Hence, when you fight the good fight of faith, declare God's Word to that devil, situation, or circumstance as the absolute authority. Be bold, resolute, and fearless.

Dear child of God, if you ever find yourself in a position where you try to reason or rationalize God's instructions or command to you, know for certain that is the devil trying to entice you to sin and disobedience. He intends to take you out of

God's will and purpose for your life and disconnect you from the blessings of salvation.

A lot of times, people want God's results their way, not God's way and if they can't employ their own methods or techniques, they get offended. Remember Naaman, the great Syrian commander? He was given simple instructions for his healing from leprosy. He became angry because he had preconceived notions for his healing. He thought his ways were better than God's. If he had gone ahead to bathe in the rivers of Damascus which he preferred to the Jordan river, he would have denied himself a tremendous miracle. (2 kings 5:9-14).

Understanding the Gospel
What is the Gospel? A lot of people just summarize the Gospel as being the Word of God. It is much more than that. It is God's message concerning the person, mission, and redemptive works of Jesus Christ. It is God's offer of eternal life. If you fully understand this, you are set on the course of victory and consistent progress. In Mark 4:15, Jesus refereed to the seeds that fell by the wayside. The word was indeed sown in their hearts but because

of a lack of understanding, the devil snatched them away.

"Wisdom is the principal thing; therefore, get wisdom: and with all thy getting get understanding" Proverbs 4:7.

No matter how valid your pursuits are in life, only the understanding and application of God's Word will give you the advantage and put you ahead in life. As a child of God who wants to consistently make progress in life, you must know your God and do His Word. For the people who know their God shall be strong and do exploits (Daniel 11:32).

Jesus learnt obedience through what he suffered (Hebrews 5:8). Contrary to some opinions, suffering (hardship, pressures, frustrations, betrayal, and defeat) doesn't take you out of obedience, it rather produces in you the fruits of obedience and patience.

In 1 Peter 1:14, God calls you obedient children. As a born-again Christian, obedience is your nature so, live in submission to God's Word and the direction of the Holy Spirit. Resolve that nothing shall separate you from the love of God that is in Christ Jesus (Romans 8:39).

CHAPTER 4

ANOTHER GOSPEL

Then the serpent said to the woman, "You will not surely die. For God knows that in the day you eat of it your eyes will be opened, and you will be like God, knowing good and evil." (Genesis 3:4-5)

As we have seen, there is a perversion of wisdom (a falsification) designed to work against the pure and simple Word of God. That perversion is the artfulness and deceitfulness of the serpent.

The serpent can have the appearance of wisdom (Matthew 10:16) and the semblance of light (2 Corinthians 11:14a) which is why deception is possible.

Why is wisdom attributed to the serpent as seen in Matthew 10:16? The serpent is a very sharp-sighted, cunning creature, and uses various arts and stratagems for its preservation and attack.

"Dan shall be a serpent by the way, an adder in the path, that biteth the horse heels, so that his rider shall fall backwards". Genesis 49:17

The above scripture describes the nature of the serpent. It hides in the path. It is not easily discerned, it is often trampled unawares, and bites at once unexpected. It gains its conquests principally by surprise, cunning and art than valor.

Eve fell prey to the cunning and deceitfulness of the serpent hence justified her disobedience by tagging the forbidden as "good for food, pleasant to the eyes and desirable to make one wise". Sin becomes justifiable or even reasonable, good, pleasant, and harmless when one is misled or deceived by Satan.

*"So when the woman saw that **the tree** was **good for food**, that it was **pleasant to the eyes**, and a tree **desirable to make one wise**, she took of its fruit and*

ate. She also gave to her husband with her, and he ate."
Genesis 3:6-7.

The evil dialogue between the woman and the serpent, with the subsequent disobedience of Adam and Eve, happened right inside the Garden - the garden that God made specially for Adam and Eve; the garden in which was the presence of God. It is important to note that the serpent did not lure Eve out of the garden but worked his deception right inside the Garden where Adam and Eve were both created, were given a divine assignment, and enjoyed daily a rich fellowship with God Himself.

The devil dared to slither into their dwelling, the place of fellowship, communion, and intimacy with God; and spun his web of lies and deception that trapped them both. It is important to stay on your guard no matter where you are and what you do. Don't say I am a highly esteemed and renowned pastor, I am a professional with years of experience, I have the best hands in business or governance. Stay alert! Be vigilant!

"Be sober, be vigilant; because your adversary the devil, as a roaring lion, walketh about, seeking whom he may devour" 1 Peter 5:8

The lion may be the strongest animal, but it never attacks a herd head-on. It usually attacks from the rear. If all the animals are together and keep pace, it cannot attack. The lion stalks the herd, watching out for the weak and injured animals that cannot keep up with the herd, and these constitute its prey. So do not sleep on your watch. Be fervent in spirit. Never stray from God's perfect will for your life at any point.

Remember Samson became careless and was trapped by the wiles of Delilah. Samson knew he was special, and God's hand was mighty on him, but he became presumptuous. When the Philistines came upon him, he said *"I will go out as other times and shake myself. And he wist not that the Lord was departed from him"* Judges 16:20.

Observe the subtlety of Delilah. She made him sleep upon her knees. Samson was destroyed where he felt most secure. And he did not even realize that the power had left him when he awoke, until he perceived a threat. Sadly, many have lost the fellowship of the Holy Spirit and are not even aware of it. They have provoked God to withdraw and are not even sensible to it.

Another instance of a great man who got careless is recorded in the fourth chapter of Judges. Sisera was the captain of the Canaan army under king Jabin.

Like Samson, he was taken unawares. The bible records that he fell asleep in a woman's tent in the thick of battle. He trusted the woman so much and felt so secure in her tent that he fell fast asleep. So, he died, not in the field of battle, but in a tent; not by the sword but by a nail; not by the hand of a warrior but of a woman. *"Wherefore let him that thinketh he standeth take heed lest he fall". 1 Corinthians10:12,*

Dear child of God, the devil will always employ very subtle means so that disobedience is usually justifiable. Moses had his reasons to hit the rock with his staff instead of speaking to it as God commanded him. King Saul had reason to take the fat cattle and sheep instead of destroying them as God instructed them. Judas had his reason to betray Jesus. They were all successful in carrying out Satan's enterprise, but they all suffered devastating consequences.

This is all that I have learned: God made us plain and simple, **but we have made ourselves very complicated.** *(Ecclesiastes 7:29 GNT)*

Fear or Love?
Our submission and obedience to God's Word should not be from fear of reprisal or punishment but out of love.

Indeed, God made it clear to Adam and Eve from the onset that they would die if they transgressed, but you should know that God sometimes may give an instruction or command without notification of the consequences. God did not warn Moses of the consequences of hitting the rock, but he was punished. Do you really think that if God had given Moses any indication that he would not enter the promised land, that he would have acted foolishly? Most likely not!

"I pray thee, let me go over, and see the good land that is beyond Jordan, that goodly mountain and Lebanon". Deuteronomy 3:25.

Notwithstanding Moses' very earnest prayer and God's love and special favor towards him, he was not permitted to enter the promised land.

For I earnestly protested to and warned your fathers at the time that I brought them up out of the land of Egypt, even to this day, protesting to and warning them persistently, saying, Obey My voice. Jeremiah 11:7 AMP.

Dear Friend, God's instruction to you should suffice. Do not be the one who will heed instruction only for fear of penalties. The love of Christ should constrain, motivate, and inspire to obedience and the discharge of our duty to Him, as well as keep you from walking in defiance and disobedience.

Another gospel
"I marvel that ye are so soon removed from him that called you into the grace of Christ unto another gospel:

which is not another; but there be some that trouble you and would pervert the gospel of Christ". Galatians 1:6-7

The word gospel is from the Greek word *evangelion* meaning "good tidings" or "good news". So, another gospel should mean another good news. But then, how good is the news?

In the above text, the apostles used the term "another gospel" to represent the false teachings because it opened and offered a different way of justification and salvation from that which was revealed in Christ's authentic Gospel.

At face value, another gospel may portend good and even appear worthy of acceptance as truth, but the end thereof is destruction of lives and a breakdown of society.

Today, there are many spurious gospels in circulation. These are a perversion of the true Gospel and sadly is preached from the pulpits and have been woven into the very fabric of faith and worship in some places of worship.

Jesus said in Matthew 24:14 *"And this gospel of the kingdom shall be preached in all the world for a witness unto all nation; and then shall the end come"*.

Observe the Lord didn't say "the Gospel" but "**this Gospel**". He was referring to a specific Gospel, the Gospel of the kingdom which He Himself preached. There is but one pure Gospel of the grace of God and Christ. There is not one and another; only one pure Gospel. The Gospel is single and uniform. It has no contradictions in it. It cannot be edited, reviewed, or updated.

Jesus brought good news, a testimony of His finished redemptive works and eternal life for man. This good news brings people to salvation and to live in obedience to God. Another gospel also has promises but never brings about true salvation and obedience to God.

Galations1:7 makes a strong categorization of all false and inaccurate renditions: *"which is not another"*. This means contrary to opinion; it is no Gospel and no good news. It may be called a gospel, but it differs most essentially from the authentic Gospel of the kingdom.

There are those who accept the wrong doctrine because it is endorsed and preached by an esteemed, respected, and renowned minister, or one in whom they have confidence. Because of this, many have been led astray.

The uprightness of a person does not validate or authenticate his teaching.

Remember the Berean Jews? They searched the scriptures daily to corroborate the message the apostles preached. They did not just take the message hook, line, and sinker because it was preached by apostle Paul.

"But though we, or an angel from heaven preach any other Gospel unto you than that which we have preached unto you; let him be accursed." Galatians 1:8.

"If there arises among you a prophet or a dreamer of dreams, and he gives you a sign or a wonder, and the sign or the wonder comes to pass, of which he spoke to

you, saying, 'Let us go after other gods' — which you have not known — 'and let us serve them,' you shall not listen to the words of that prophet or that dreamer of dreams, for **the Lord your God is testing you to know whether you love the Lord your God with all your heart and with all your soul.** *You shall walk after the Lord your God and fear Him and* **keep His commandments and obey His voice**; *you shall serve Him and hold fast to Him."* Deuteronomy 13:1-5.

Child of God do not be gullible. Refuse to remain at the level of a child. Attain maturity in Christ and know the Word of God for yourself.

"That we henceforth be no more children, tossed to and fro, and carried about with every wind of doctrine, by the sleight of men, and cunning craftiness, whereby they lie in wait to deceive." Ephesians 4:14.

The Jewish leaders, to distort the truth of Christ's resurrection, bribed the soldiers to say that His disciples stole His body at night. *"So they took the money, and did as they were taught: and this saying is commonly reported among the Jews until this day."* Matthew 28:15.

Can you imagine that! After 2000 years, the lies and deception are still being circulated, believed, and acted on.

Let's examine closely some teachings that are believed today in Christendom:

Example 1. The true Gospel from the Lord Jesus Christ says, "Love your enemies, and pray for those who persecute you."(Matthew 5:44 GNT

Another gospel says "Don't let your enemies live. Kill them before they kill you. Any enemy that says you will not live and enjoy the fruits of your labor; what are you waiting for? Die!" This other gospel has shaped the prayers of many Christians today who engage in this form of prayer in defense against human enemies.

Well, at first when this type of prayer was introduced in the body of Christ, the understanding was that it was not intended for a physical enemy but the spirit behind the enemy, forgetting that spirits don't die. Why then is death incorporated into the prayer and made the subject?

Addressing the fact that spirits don't die, it was said the prayer was not for the death of the spirit but the eternal separation of the spirit. However, this has very quickly unraveled to the point where people are no longer "after" the spirit working through a person, they want their perceived enemy dead. The word "die," "kill" are now more commonly associated with a supposed enemy than the word "love." Yet the Lord Jesus expressly commanded, "love your enemies."

The Lord Jesus is our perfect example. He had enemies who not only wanted Him dead but went ahead to kill Him. Yet He never prayed for them to die rather He prayed to the Father for their forgiveness instead.

Some people insist that God still hears and answers such prayers. They argue that If God doesn't want to eliminate those who trouble them, why then does He answer such prayers?
There are things one may do in the Name of God, which are contrary to His perfect will, but would still yield the desired results. Moses acting in

disobedience, struck the rock and water still came out of the rock.

Hear this! Your great and even supernatural results are not God's endorsement of your actions. Those that Jesus categorized as workers of iniquity in Matthew 7:22, did many wonderful and supernatural works (cast out devils and prophesied amongst other things) in the Name of Jesus but they did not end well.

The plan of the devil through "another gospel" is to make the true Gospel look weak and impotent. For one may reason, how can loving your enemy solve the problem of your enemy wanting you dead? It would make more sense to eliminate the enemy rather than be eliminated.

Ask the right questions
God is not against asking the right questions. Mary the mother of Jesus and Gideon asked questions and got answers. For instance, you can ask the right question by faith "How can loving an enemy preserve one from his wicked plans and schemes?" You will receive the right answer from the Holy

Spirit, as well as God's strategy and guidance to disarm the one who opposes you.

The Lord Jesus admonishes us to be wise as serpents. In your dealings with people, and in relationships, let God's wisdom guide you. A lot of people are hurt in relationships because they trust too easily. They equate love with trust. Nowhere in the bible does Jesus instruct us to trust man. The command is for us to love. The Lord gave His life for mankind out of love, but never entrusted Himself to man (John 2:24). He knows the heart of man.

Dear friend, love your enemies, pray for them to come to the knowledge of the truth, but never trust any man. Remember what misplaced trust did to Samson and Sisera.

Example 2 The true Gospel says, bless those who curse you (Luke 6:28). Another gospel says" back to sender".

Some may wonder "How do I bless my enemies? Is it so that they can prosper in their wickedness? I was asked this question once, while I was teaching in a Sunday school class.

"Who, when he was reviled, reviled not again; when he suffered, he threatened not; but committed himself to him that judgeth righteously" 1 Peter 2:23.

This is an example and instruction to Christians to do likewise; not to seek revenge but to leave our course with God who is in His own time, will avenge the wrong and injuries done His saints.

Let us take it a step further and look at what Jesus was anointed to do in the book of Luke 4:18-19. From there, we can list out the blessings we can proclaim upon our enemies and indeed upon anyone we want saved. This includes:

- For the Gospel to reach them
- For their broken hearts to be healed
- To be set free from the captivity of the devil
- To recover their sight and be free from blindness
- To be free from satanic oppression
- To turn their hearts from darkness to light and from the dominion of Satan unto God

Example 3: The issue of Holy Ghost fire
The scripture says Jesus will baptize us with the Holy Ghost and with fire (Matthew 3:11). This is the true Gospel. Every believer should seek to be baptized with the Holy Ghost and with fire. The fire was the "cloven tongues '.

Jesus said to the disciples "and you shall receive power, after that the Holy Ghost is come upon you". (Acts 1:8)

The cloven tongues of fire were the symbol of the power and extraordinary gifts of the Spirit. When the disciples received the baptism of the Holy Ghost, the power they didn't have before came upon them instantly. The disciples were no longer ordinary men, they received the Holy Ghost and fire upon them. Soul winning became easy and effective with resultant great numerical growth in the church.

"Another gospel" combined the two words to form "Holy Ghost Fire," which for them is God's weapon of mass destruction. There is no phrase like Holy Ghost Fire in the bible. What you have is "with the Holy Ghost and with Fire". Jesus never, upon any occasion use the phrase Holy Ghost fire nor called for fire from heaven as a means of destruction, and neither did the apostles. So how did it originate?

The bible records that the prophet Elijah called fire from heaven and that was in the Old Testament. Jesus rebuked His disciples for referring to the acts of Elijah and attempting to employ a similar technique for punishing the Samaritans, the enemies of Christ.
(Luke 9:54-55). This, Jesus explained to them is not the spirit of the Gospel dispensation.

The phrase "Holy Ghost fire" is an invention outside the truth of the bible, and a distortion of reality.

The original wording is Holy Ghost and fire: a baptism we are meant to experience from the Lord to make us bold and full of power to preach the Gospel and demonstrate the supernatural ability of God's Spirit.

Any distortion of God's word has a satanic goal. Why seek for the baptism of the Holy Ghost when you can shout Holy Ghost fire? Shouting Holy Ghost fire produces faster results? Do you really think so?

Jesus never instructed His disciples to use the technique of shouting Holy Ghost Fire to neutralize the works of darkness. Jesus said, "in My Name, they shall cast out devils" Mark 16:17. Everything in heaven, on earth and beneath the earth bows to the Name of Jesus. In dealing with demons, Jesus never screamed or became hysterical. With a simple command, the devils obeyed. Moreover, in Ephesians 6, where we are trained on the ammunitions for warfare, nowhere is the Holy Ghost fire mentioned.

There are those who say it yields results, but the end does not always justify the means. The fact that you may get results does not also mean that you are aligned with God's perfect will and that God is pleased with it. Again, remember Moses? He got the same result striking the rock when God specifically ordered him to speak to it. He paid dearly for that foolishness.

As a babe in Christ, the Lord may permit or allow some things, but at a certain point, He expects you to put away childish things.
When I was a child, I spake as a child, I understood as a child, I thought as a child: but when I became a man, I put away childish things. 1 Corinthians 13:11.

Benefits of the baptism with the Holy Spirit.
For some, the only evidence in their lives of being baptized with the Holy Ghost is that they speak in new tongues. I am glad you speak in tongues but let me point out that you did not receive the Holy Ghost just to speak in new tongues.

"......And they were all filled with the Holy Ghost, and they spake the Word of God with boldness" Acts 4:31

When you have the Holy Ghost, you receive boldness to win souls and power to heal the sick and cast out devils. You cannot receive the Holy Ghost and live an ordinary, lack luster life.

Speaking in tongue is for personal edification (1 Corinthians 14:4). As important as it is, to produce the same results that the disciples produced, you will agree that there is something more than speaking in tongues that is required.

The bible records that the works that Jesus did testified of Him, not His prayers or quiet time. He said in John 14:11 believe me for the very works sake. If you have the Holy Ghost, your works should speak.

Operating in the gifts of the Spirit should never replace your submission to the direction and leading of the Holy Spirit. There is a common occurrence among some believers. Upon receipt of a spiritual gift from the Lord, they may tend to build an ecosystem around that gift. This is good, the challenge is that our attention to the gift may become a distraction.

The disciples received the Holy Ghost, and starting from Jerusalem, were supposed to spread out with the Gospel to other regions, instead they remained in Jerusalem with what they had received. It took persecution to scatter them.

For every accomplishment and fulfillment, there is always more with God. 1 Corinthians 12:31 asserts that we covet earnestly the best gifts – prophesying, teaching, doing miracles, interpreting different tongues, healing the sick. Gifts that are the most useful and beneficial to the church. If you speak in tongues presently, fervently desire to do more.

"Most assuredly, I say to you, he who believes in Me, the works that I do he will do also; ***and greater works than these he will do****, because I go to My Father. John 14:12.*

EVIL AWARENESS

"For God knows that in the day you eat of it your eyes will be opened, and you will be like God, knowing good and evil." (Genesis 3:5)

The opening text was the devil's trump card. He sold a lie and deception to Eve, and she fell for it artlessly. She was captivated by the possibility of being like God when the truth is she, as well as Adam were already made in the image and likeness of God. If she fully understood the truth, she would have recognized the deception for what it was.

The devil was incensed against man for God had given man what he so badly wanted. (Isaiah 14:14).

When man committed high treason in Eden, his spirit became subject to his senses. Prior to this time, his knowledge was spiritual. He saw only what God saw. After the fall, Adam could see the glory no longer. He saw himself naked.

In Genesis 3:11, God asked Adam who told you that you were naked? By what means did you get this knowledge? What have you done to be sensible of being naked? Adam and Eve must have done something to have sensory perception. They did not become naked after the fall. No! they were naked all the while but were covered by God's glory. They had no business knowing they were naked. God continued His probe by asking "hast thou eaten of the tree I commanded thee that thou shoudest not eat?"

The only way Adam could be subject to the senses was because he was disconnected from God.

When the serpent asserted that even God knows that their eyes will be opened, little did they know that it was actually that their eyes would be opened to darkness and corruption.

As a child of God, you are created to see from God's perspective. You see the glory of God, His light, and His beauty. What the devil intends is that you see through the senses. This is what happened to Adam in the garden. He saw what darkness showed him, a naked and shameful condition. A disconnection from God brings about an awareness of evil.

Dear child of God, you have been completely and permanently disconnected from the corruptions and destructions of this world. 2 Corinthians 5:17 says "behold all things have become new". Not a few things or even most things but all things - your health, family, marriage, business, ministry, career. There is a word in that scripture that a lot of people overlook. Note the word "behold". This means "see". As a Christian, you have been totally and permanently disconnected from the first Adam. Refuse to see the experiences associated with the first Adam. Refuse to look at the unwholesome state of your health, business, family, marriage, or finances. Instead see the fullness of the blessings of the Gospel that is yours in Christ.

"And being not weak in faith, he considered not his own body now dead, when he was about an hundred years old, neither yet the deadness of Sarah's womb". Romans 4:19

Abrahams body did not change to that of a vibrant young man after God's promise, but he refused to contemplate his conditions. He called Himself Abraham meaning Father of many nations when as at, yet he had no son.

"He staggered not at the promise of God through unbelief, but was strong in faith, giving glory to God" Romans 4:20

Strong faith does not cry, complain, murmur, or worry but gives glory to God. Worry is futile, and dishonors God. Refuse to weep or murmur but praise Him.

Even God knows:
With this phrase, the devil insinuated that God was holding back something that was good and beneficial to Adam and Eve. That God was unwilling that they should enjoy something desirable and endeavored to prevent it by the prohibition.

Let's take another look at Eve. With all the trees in the garden which she could enjoy, she was drawn to the one tree that God said they could not enjoy.

Amidst all God's blessings in your life, the devil always tries to draw you to the one thing you may not presently enjoy: that one unfulfilled desire. Many times, we may yearn for that "one tree" to the exclusion of all others. For instance, a young unmarried woman who is blessed with beauty, good health, a fantastic job, a good home, a car, a solid circle of friends etc. The devil may come to her and whisper "even God knows you are fully matured and should be in your husband's house. See all your younger sisters are married and they do not serve God as faithfully as you do." Such a one may begin to fret about her unmarried state instead of giving glory to God.

The devil is a very subtle adversary. Before God, he is the accuser of the brethren. Before the saints, he accuses God. The devil will attempt to indict God of not being loving or faithful enough. All of this occurs in the mind.

Child of God, the mind is a battlefield. Today the serpent will not engage you physically but will slither into your mind filling you with negative thoughts, images and reasonings. You may think, these are just thoughts but that is how the devil operates, through your mind. These thoughts, if allowed to linger, bring doubts and fear. The devil will always attempt to bring you to the point where you believe God is holding back something or is being deliberately unresponsive.

Now the serpent was more cunning than any beast of the field which the Lord God had made. And he said to the woman, "Has God indeed said, 'You shall not eat of every tree of the garden'?" Genesis 3:1.

Once a man gives heed to the deception of the devil, he disregards godly instructions and commits sin.

How do you deal with the negative thoughts, lies and deceptions of Satan? Let us refer to the ammunition listed in Ephesians 6. The negative thoughts and images, the discouragement, procrastination, anxiety, fear, shame, depression are all the fiery darts of the enemy. The bible says we use the shield of faith "to quench all the fiery darts of the wicked". A dart signifies any kind of missile weapon; everything that is projected to a distance by the hand e.g., a javelin, spear, or an arrow. They are referred to as fiery darts because they sometimes come suddenly and swiftly and thick and fast. When they hit the target, can be very grievous.

We are told the weapons of our warfare are mighty through God to the pulling down of satanic strongholds. The shield of faith is effective against all satanic incursions and can extinguish any fiery attack. We are instructed to take up the shield of faith. A shield is of no use to a warrior if it is not in the hand of the warrior. Likewise, the Word of God is not effective if it is not in your mouth: declared, verbalized, spoken, vocalized. So, take up the Word of God. Keep your faith filled declarations in your mouth. Jesus countered every attack vocally. Likewise keep talking the Word. Use the Word against fear, doubt, anxiety and neutralize them.
When Peter, in faith, walked on water, it was a supernatural and glorious experience. When he saw the wind, he began to sink. The sinking experience was never part of what the Master intended for him to experience when He gave the command "come". The sinking became part of Peter's story because of fear. It's funny though, till

date, whenever this account of Peter is given, people always remember and emphasize the sinking which was never supposed to have occurred.

For I know the thoughts that I think toward you, saith the Lord, thoughts of peace, and not of evil, to give you an expected end. Jeremiah 29:11.

God prepared for you in Christ. His plans are plans of life, health, success, prosperity, peace, security, glory; all the things that are consistent with the death, burial, and resurrection of Christ Jesus. As a Christian, the path you walk in life is God-ordained and there is no death, sickness, or disease on that path. So why does the Christian have experiences that are at variance with God's plan? There are certain contrary occurrences that were never part of the story or journey of our lives, but they showed up because of a lack of knowledge or an act of disobedience.

"...whoso breaketh an hedge, a serpent shall bit him." Ecclesiastes 10:8. Simply put, the text above means

whoever transgress God's commands, will suffer for it.

When David disobeyed God, he opened the door for untold horrors. His son Absalom was intent on killing David and usurping the kingdom. The same Absalom slept with his father's wives in public view. David's children committed incest. All manner of evil and so much pain unleashed on the family because of David's disobedience.

Uprightness and right standing with God (moral and spiritual rectitude in every area and relation) elevate a nation, but sin is a reproach to any people. Proverbs 14:34 AMP.

Today, we experience indescribable evil in our society: fraud, terrorism, kidnapping, ritualism, prostitution, homosexuality. There is break down of order and authority. The leaders have no clue how to rectify the problems. Young men and women who were good citizens have become lawless and wicked all in a bid to "survive". There is no longer value for a human life. Who are those that have broken the hedge and opened the portals for all these evil in our society?

Some people have sustained huge losses; lost their marriages, jobs, resources due to disobedience.

The first time I got defrauded was by a traditional ruler. He promised to award me a community project; one I had the capacity to execute. He said the community had an agreement with an oil company to install solar streetlights in the community. Since that was part of my field of expertise, he requested that I submit a proposal for the job, which I did. Prior to this time, I had received a prophecy of some major financial breakthrough, so I assumed that this was it and I did not diligently seek God's face on the matter.

The traditional ruler demanded money from me to be paid in instalments, for "mobilization and consultation with the elders". By this time, I had already started getting some signal in my spirit that something was not right. Regrettably I disregarded the signal because of the "prophecy" as well as the expected revenue. I also trusted the traditional ruler because of his elevated status in society. But I realized after I had made the first payment that I had been duped. I pulled out of the transaction immediately and understood later that many others had lost vast sums of money because of this scheme.

I have experienced firsthand the crushing disappointments and the frustrations of being duped but I could have spared myself that experience if I heeded the promptings of the Holy Spirit. I thank God, I quit when I did. The loss would have been a great deal more substantial.

When Peter began to sink, he cried unto the Lord saying: "Lord, save me!" (Mathew 14:30). And the scripture records that the Lord "immediately" reached out and pulled him up. When you get into problems, learn to cry unto God for help immediately. Do not justify or rationalize "your sinking". Do not shift blame or indulge in self-pity. Repent immediately. Take responsibility for your actions or lack thereof and call on the Lord for help.

Look retrospectively, what in your life may provide room for the enemy to challenge God's Word in your life? What represents that "one tree" for you: a strong but unfulfilled desire? What situation or challenge has taunted you for so long? Is it a health condition, a financial downturn, marital problems? Refuse to listen to every contrary voice of doubt and fear. Do not walk in disobedience or contrary to God's will. Maintain your confession of God's Word over that situation giving glory to God.

Child of God, remember that surely there is an end to that situation and your expectations shall be fulfilled. Amen!

Child of God, remember, Jesus was tempted in every respect as we are yet without sinning. He too was confronted by contrary situations and circumstances of life but continued to "walk on water". He walked in absolute dominion and mastery. If Jesus did not "sink", neither should we.

Jesus is our perfect example. We must learn from Him, and live like Him. That way we get the same results He had, and nothing shall be impossible with us.

CHAPTER 6

THE KINGDOM FIRST

"But seek first the kingdom of God and His righteousness and all these things shall be added unto you" (Matthew 6:33)

As a Christian, it is your duty to desire and seek the furtherance of God's kingdom.

It is observable that every stage or phase of life is a quest to attain a goal: seeking an education, seeking a job or position, seeking a partner, seeking happiness. For some, it has become an allconsuming pursuit to the exclusion of everything else. The driving force or motivation for this quest is the world's standard or definition of success for every level in life. Sadly, many Christians have been sucked into this frenetic vortex.

For after all these things do the Gentiles seek: for your heavenly Father knoweth that ye have need of all these things. Matthew 6:32.

The Lord Jesus did not mince words when He said, "for after all these things do the gentiles seek" (Luke 12:30), further clarifies "Gentiles" as nations of the world. The Gentiles are those who do not know God. They greedily seek after, and are anxiously concerned for food, clothes, houses, cars, and riches. For them the end justifies the means and so will employ any means, fair or foul. Sadly, there are those who are Christians who are more concerned about worldly affairs than the interests of the kingdom.

Now the ones that fell among thorns are those who, when they have heard, go out and are choked with cares, riches, and pleasures of life, and bring no fruit to maturity. Luke 8:14.

The hearers described here are those who after hearing, go forth to their worldly business or go on in their worldly pursuits – seeking those things that the Gentiles seek. They are entangled with the cares, riches, and pleasures of this world. For these, riches become a snare rather than a blessing. Such do not see the relevance of submitting to a divine authority believing all they have was gotten by their power. They consider themselves already successful: rich and healthy, so do not recognize the value of the blessings of the Gospel.

God never planned that the Christian be part of that rat race, for in Christ, God has already given you all you require for life and godliness.

But ye (yes YOU) are a chosen generation, a royal priesthood, an holy nation, a peculiar people; that ye should show shew forth the praises of him who hath called you out of darkness into His marvelous light) 1 Peter
2:9 (Emphasis mine)

The sooner you understand that you are different, the better for you. You play by a different set of rules, and it is expected that your results should be glaringly different. The opening text establishes for us a divine decree, method, and arrangement. Be mindful of the order: seek **first** the kingdom of God and His righteousness. In the opening text, there is a word whose significance has been downplayed and sometimes even ignored but it is the thread that ties that instruction together. It is the crux of the instruction or order.

Jesus said seek FIRST. Not after! Not at your convenience, or in your time! There is a vast difference between the two instructions, "seek ye the kingdom of God" and "seek ye first the kingdom of God". The Greek word rendered "first" here is the word *proton*. It means first in time or place, in any succession of things or persons. The word "first" gives the task of seeking the kingdom top priority and preeminence. It denotes an order or sequence. You get the blessings only when you seek the kingdom FIRST. A lot of people become frustrated, discontented, tired, and discouraged simply because that which should come first has been given subordinate attention.

Child of God, get the order right! You cannot get God's results your way. God will certainly not alter or modify the order for you; but will, if you ask Him, give you the wisdom to get it right.

When you put God's kingdom first, the free bounty, goodness, and liberality of God is yours without your thought and care and much less your merit. In other words, you get to enjoy life without struggle, frustration, and anxiety.

So, get your priorities right. If what you are doing, or giving attention and priority to, does not promote the interests of the kingdom of God first and foremost, disengage from it.

In 2 Chronicles 1:11-12, Solomon got the order right. He put the first things, first. He did not ask God for riches, wealth, honor, or victory over his enemies but wisdom. There is nothing bad in having riches, wealth, honor etc. It is all about prioritization or ranking. When you seek the kingdom first, you will receive wisdom to better manage, utilize and enjoy the blessings of God. God gave Solomon all the things he did not even ask for. When he received all the blessings, he did not abuse the riches, honor, and glory as long as he centered on God. He had established the right order.

Our life here on earth is a function of time. What you give your time to, controls your life. If you give the kingdom of God priority in your life, the kingdom of God will regulate your life, protect, and promote you, as well as make provisions for you. It's really that simple.

The interest of God's kingdom is to promote righteousness, therefore if the business ethics in a company is not in line with the kingdom principles, you ought not work there. Your first watch word should be righteousness in your dealings, relationships, and transactions.

God sent the prophet Elijah to a widow of Zarephath in a time of famine. She was not a rich widow with ample resources but a poor widow who did not have enough for herself and her son. Upon Elijah's request for food, she responded that she was preparing the last meal for her and her son. One would think that the prophet would be moved with compassion, withdraw his request, and probably look for a way to augment her meagre ration, instead he said, *"Make me thereof a little cake **first**, and bring it unto me, and **after** make for thee and for thy son."* 1 Kings 17:13.

The prophet made a demand on the small pittance requisite to keep the widow's child from dying. One would imagine the prophet's request was rather extreme. He did not even request that he eat with the family but insisted that he be served first and then the widow could prepare food for herself and her son. It was a great trial of her faith in God and her obedience. Because she obeyed God and served the prophet first, God commanded His blessing on the flour and oil. If she had prepared food for herself and her son first, there would have been none left for the divine blessing to descend upon.

There are times when the needs seem to overwhelm the available resources. Because the needs are so valid and urgent, the temptation arises to jettison the kingdom and focus on the areas requiring very urgent attention. It is important to let the wisdom of God direct you in making the right financial choices and decisions in life.

Remember, the widow had genuine needs, but she also had a choice. If she had insisted on taking care of her needs first, she would have died. She obeyed God and lived in surplus.

Then Peter began to say to Him, "See, we have left all and followed you." So Jesus answered and said, "Assuredly, I say to you, there is no one who has left house or brothers or sisters or father or mother or wife or children or lands, for My sake and the gospel's, who shall not receive a hundredfold now in this time — houses and brothers and sisters and mothers and children and lands, with persecutions — and in the age to come, eternal life." Mark 10:28-30.

Dear friend, nothing you do for the kingdom is useless. Every investment in the kingdom not only has its reward here on earth but is also of eternal value.
Therefore, my beloved brethren, be ye stedfast, unmovable, always abounding in the work of the Lord, forasmuch as ye know that your labour is not in vain in the Lord. 1Corinthians 15:58.

The winning strategy:
The life of the kingdom is not about experiencing good or abstaining from evil. It is about living the God life, the supernatural and superior life of God in the human body. It is about exercising the dominion and authority of Christ over your world, as well as harnessing God's lavish blessings to promote His work and impact lives.

Experiencing troubles or adversity does not mean you have derailed as a Christian or that you no longer please God. A thousand times no! Sometimes God allows the challenges so you can demonstrate His authority and win in life. Adversity is not the issue but your response to it will determine the results you get.

The bible says count it all joy when ye fall into diverse temptations.

James 1:2. Why should we rejoice whenever we encounter trials of any sort? These challenges present avenues for promotion. They are the necessary exams by which we are promoted to the next and higher level of life.

On the flip side, your enjoyment of bodily and material prosperity may not always indicate that you are in total alignment with God's will and plan for your life. One may argue that experiencing "all the things the Gentiles seek" is an indication that God is pleased with the order of their priorities in life. A lot of people have erroneously used the world's standards or symbols of success to measure God's acceptance of them.

But he said to her, "You speak as one of the foolish women speaks. Shall we indeed accept good from God, and shall we not accept adversity?" **In all this Job did not sin with his lips.** *Job 2:10.*

There are those who have done all they know to do during trials and adversity. They pray, study God's Word, remain diligent in service and yet they struggle. Sometimes they lash out at God as the disciples did *"is it nothing to you that we are going down" Mark 4:38* The Message translation.

Dear child of God, as Joyce Meyer succinctly puts it, the problem is right under your nose. The question is, **what are you saying?**

Job in all his suffering and afflictions did not sin with his lips- he did not murmur or complain. **He let no wrong word escape from his lips.** Do you know that your tongue steers your life? It can steer you out of any trouble as well as put you in troubled waters.

For in many things we offend all. If any man offend not in word, the same is a perfect man, and able to bridle the whole body. James 3:2

From the above text we see that our utterances regulate our lives. Train yourself to speak words that are consistent with God's Word. The bible says you shall have whatsoever you say. Begin to place a premium on your words.

For he that will love life, and see good days, let him refrain his tongue from evil, and his lips that they speak no guile. 1 Peter 3:10

Paraphrased the text means speaking only in conformity with God's Word. Do not let bad things happen to you. Speak the right words irrespective of the circumstances.

Prosperity is your birthright
Beloved, I wish above all things that thou mayest prosper and be in health, even as thy soul prospereth. 3 John 1:2

It is important to be filled with the knowledge of God's precise at every point in time. Indeed, God expects us to prioritize and put the kingdom first as we have been instructed in Matthew 6:33. This, however, does not eliminate the place of material blessings and comforts in life. In the preceding verse, the bible tells us *"For your heavenly Father knoweth that ye have need of all these things.*

What things exactly? It includes but is not limited to what you will eat, drink and wear. We can further expand it to include where you will live, school, work, occupation, etc. It is important to note that God knows that you **need ALL** these things. Therefore, even God considers them essential, necessities and prerequisite for life. It is therefore erroneous to look down on or abhor the blessings that are added to you when you seek the kingdom of God. Remember God added to Solomon wealth, riches, and honour. Do not take the scripture out of context. The scripture says seek first not seek only. When you put God's kingdom first, "all these things" which you do not seek, will come to you of a free course unhindered. Do not be oblivious to this truth.

So, does God want you rich and prosperous? A thousand times yes! Your prosperity is needed to promote the Gospel. Remember the Gospel is free but not cheap. The Lord said in Zechariah 1:17, "My cities through prosperity shall be spread abroad". Whose prosperity was God referring to? The prosperity of His saints of course! God expects us to use our God-given resources to promote the work of the kingdom.

The bible is replete with stories of wicked men who used their resources and positions to advance a satanic agenda:

- Haman proposed to give king Ahasuerus ten thousand talents of silver to exterminate the Jews.
- Judas received thirty pieces of silver to betray Jesus.
- The chief priests and elders offered soldiers large sums of money to lie that the disciples had stolen the body of Jesus thereby spreading doubts on the resurrection of Christ.

Today, there are those who have given their seats (positions, offices, authority) to Satan and are using their resources to promote and finance an antichrist agenda to destroy lives, livelihoods, and the sovereignty of nations.

As children of God, we can't stop at prayer alone. We need to invest in the kingdom of God and overthrow the works of darkness.

God also requires and places His children in positions of great political and financial influence to establish His righteousness. Remember God had to position Joseph as the number two man in Egypt so His will for Israel could be done. Joseph could never have wielded that degree of relevance and influence as Potiphar's steward or as a favored prisoner.

So go ahead. Aspire! Dream! Work hard but ensure that furthering the kingdom God and His righteousness is your inspiration.

There was a certain man called Joseph of Arimathea whom the bible described as rich. He went to Pilate and asked for the body of Jesus and Pilate granted his request. Jesus had earthly parents, brothers, sisters, disciples, people who loved Him and who had benefitted tremendously from His ministry. Why did none of them step up to address Pilate? Remember Jesus' death was that of a vile offender. He was killed like a condemned criminal and His body belonged to the state. It took a rich and influential man to sway the government of the day and cared for and dignify the body of Jesus.

Dear child of God do not be deceived to think that God does not need you educated or gainfully employed. The unbelievers are investing in the education of their children so that they could secure influential positions in society and make decisions that will affect millions of people. Do not sit on your oars. Do not become slothful or laid-back. It is not wrong to be ambitious. The question is, does your ambition align with God's plan and agenda? Stop giving excuses! Get up and get an education! Secure that job! Start that business! Refuse to be a spectator in the kingdom. Be relevant.

When I got my sales Job with a multinational firm, I was not thinking about it, never planned for it, and never applied for it. The offer came to me while I busied myself with what God had assigned me to do at the time. Imagine that! An offer that was open only to one person in Nigeria and West Africa at large, came to me on a platter of gold. It was because I was aligned with God's plan for my life. I was doing that which I was supposed to do. And I observed that my previous jobs prepared and qualified me for the new job. God is a master planner.

It is pertinent to note that "seeking first the kingdom of God" is not a one-off exercise. It does not have a timeline to think that you will be done with it first, then face other matters. It is ongoing through every stage and phase of your life- whether you are studying, working, in business or seeking political office. No matter what you are involved in, the kingdom is pivotal. Therefore, it would be wrong to think that you will not get an education or take an exam or get a job when the time is right, just because you are seeking the kingdom. Seeking the kingdom first does not mean you playdown or neglect the other essentials of life.

For you recall our hard toil and struggles, brethren. We worked night and day (and plied our trade) in order not to be a burden to any of you (for our support) ***while we*** *proclaimed the glad tidings (the Gospel) of God to you.* I Thessalonians 2:9 Amp.

Nor did we eat anyone's bread without paying for it, but with toil and struggle we worked night and day, that we might not be a burden or impose on any of you (for our support). It was not because we do not have a right (to such support), but we wished to make ourselves an example for you to follow. 2 Thessalonians 3:8-9. Amp.

Paul and disciples did their secular work *while* they preached. It was apparent however that the kingdom matters took preeminence over their trade. It is important to note also that their secular work did not clash with, but rather promoted the kingdom work. As you align with God's agenda and timing, do not despise other essential areas of your life that should also promote the kingdom – education, health, career, relationships, finance. You require these to function well in life and yes, in ministry.

Manage the additions:
After one year working with a multinational company, covering the West African market, in the

capacity of head, sales, there was need to recruit additional personnel. The first person I recommended for the job was a lady I met on LinkedIn. From the onset, I knew she was right for the job though she almost missed the opportunity because she did not take the offer seriously. She felt it came too easy, without all the hassles and stress of getting a good job today. It was much later when she had gotten the job that she confided in me that the job was an answer to her prayers, yet she almost turned it down because it came too easily.
There is a tendency to value and better manage the things that one has toiled for and take for granted or mismanage the things that come at no cost.

For some, whilst doing God's work, will be blessed with gifts of cars, houses, and other material blessings. Sadly, due to lack of wisdom, these blessings may become a distraction and even a snare.

Remember a man can receive nothing, except it be given him from heaven. John 3:27. Every good and perfect thing that comes to you is from God and for His glory. Learn to honor the giver, value the gift and appropriate them wisely. When God gives you a gift, remember it is not about you alone but that you might bless others as well. If you do not learn to manage what God has **added** to you, you might just lose them.

Learn from Joseph! Though he had received huge promotions and honor in Egypt, he knew it wasn't for his personal fulfillment alone. He understood that God used his position, influence and affluence "to save much people alive" Genesis 50:20.

The kingdom of God is built on spiritual principles which are expressed through physical things because we live in a physical world. We must be spiritually prepared and strategically positioned to properly harness the physical blessings that come to us.

The ministry of the Spirit

When God blesses a man, He uses another man, so human beings are the gatekeepers to these physical blessings that you need: job, promotion, education, marriage, scholarship, sponsorship, relocation to foreign lands, etc.

How does God do it so that you are singled out of a crowd and blessed beyond your connections, experience, qualifications, and contacts? It is called grace! The grace of God upon your life distinguishes you. When grace is at work in you, it brings you acceptability, favor, goodwill, promotion, protection, honor, and success. You discover that people who do not know you or even particularly like you, will bend over backwards to do you good.

For ye shall go out with joy and be led forth with peace: the mountains and the hills shall break forth before you into singing, and all the trees of the field shall clap their hands" Isaiah 55:12.

The mountains and hills refer to kings and rulers and the trees refer to people in general. God's grace makes you come into special favors with heads of governments, heads of institutions, agencies, and organizations.

Another factor that stands you out is the fruit of the Spirit.

But the fruit of the Spirit is love, joy, peace, longsuffering, gentleness, goodness, faith, meekness, temperance: against such there is no law.
Galatians 5:22-23.

Are these fully manifested in your life? Are you loving, joyful, gentle, meek, patient and kind or are you angry, spiteful, envious, irritable, ill-mannered, proud, and arrogant?

God's grace works in our lives and brings about favour, goodwill, acceptance, promotion, etc. but a wrong attitude can deprive you of these blessings and good. Do not be your own enemy. You cannot say that you have the fruit of the Spirit and yet it is hidden. The fruit finds expression in the physical and is demonstrated in relation to another person: spouse, children, family, neighbors, coworkers etc.

But now ye also put off all these; anger, wrath, malice, blasphemy, filthy communication out of your mouth.
Colossians 3:8.

Put on therefore as the elect of God, holy and beloved, bowels of mercy, kindness, humbleness of mind, meekness, longsuffering. Colossians 3:12.

Spend time meditating on God's Word. The more of God's Word stored in you, the more you are transformed by the Spirit to look and function like Jesus and get the same results.

But we all, with open face beholding as in a glass the glory of the Lord, are changed into the same image from glory to glory, even as by the Spirit of the Lord. 2 Corinthians 3:12.

Whether you require help, or you are in position to provide help, the fruit of the Spirit will make you unique, attractive, and effective.

No matter how spiritual or kingdom minded you are, it will boil down to loving God and loving your neighbors as yourself.

To be effective in your service to God and men, you are endowed with two key things:
- Gifts of the Spirit

· Fruit of the Spirit

For the gifts and calling of God are without repentance. Romans 11:29.

God never revokes or calls in His gifts. They are irreversible and immutable. They create an effective platform for you to serve others, while the fruit of the Spirit sustains you and makes you effective and productive in service.

If you have a prophetic gift for instance, the prophetic gift creates an avenue for you to function and serve as a prophet, the fruit of the Spirit enhances the quality and effectiveness of the gift. It also makes you submissive to divine direction and guidance.
The fruit of the Sprit is just as important as the gifts. Nowadays, a lot more premium is placed on gifts and the fruit is not strengthened.

Some people, due to opposition or challenges, have lost their patience, kindness, self-control, etc. but still have the gift. If you devalue the fruit of the

Spirit, you are setting yourself up for failure and defeat in life no matter the kind of gift you have.

A deep fellowship with the Holy Spirit will enhance the gifts and enrich the fruit of the Spirit. Recognize and value the person, power, and ministry of the Holy Spirit. Understand that the Holy Spirit has been given us to live the Christian life effectively. Let Him teach, direct, and guide you in all your affairs. You will live a life of no regrets.

CHAPTER 7

ABOUT GIVING, PRAYING, AND FASTING

There are many features that characterize the Christian walk. In this chapter we shall be focused on three cardinal areas: giving, praying, and fasting. These three activities are not mutually exclusive. They are not buffet items to be selected based on personal feelings or preferences. There are those who feel by doing more of one activity can compensate for the neglect of the other. For instance, one may say, my schedule does not allow me to pray much, but I am involved in giving towards church projects. In fact, I am one of the top givers in church. Congratulations! However, your giving does not replace prayer, neither does your fasting replace giving. It's like eating a lot of carbohydrates does not compensate for the functions of proteins, vitamins, or water in the body.

The Lord Jesus is our perfect model. His life is an example for us. He has given us simple instructions, and in keeping them, we would be fruitful and productive in our Christian walk and life. On the flip side, neglect or disregard of these activities and instructions about them has consequences.

God's instructions are not hard or burdensome. The Lord Jesus said my yoke is easy and my burden light. As a Christian, you have a helper and a comforter in the Holy Spirit. It is He who enables you to live a fruitful Christian life. As a matter of fact, Christianity without the Holy Spirit is mere religion. The Holy Spirit teaches, instructs, and guides us to please the Father in all things. It is He also who sanctifies your service and makes it acceptable to the Father.

Even Jesus offered Himself by the Spirit, so should we in all we do, including prayer, fasting, and giving.

God as a rewarder, creates avenues for us to be rewarded. We know that God's gifts are different from His rewards. The Gift is basically God's prerogative and doesn't depend on the receiver. Before we were born, it had been decided by God, the type of gift we should operate with. A reward on the other hand is compensation for a service.

Simple instructions on Giving:
If there is anything the devil wants to do, is to stop one from obeying God in whatever capacity and prevent one from enjoying the reward that God sets aside for obedience to His commands. Giving is what many people do virtually every week. If you don't give during the week, you give on Sunday during Sunday service. And there is a way to give to produce the result that God wants. We will not go into details in this book to begin to discuss tithe and offering, sowing seed, first fruit as subjects, and bring complexity to giving. For there

are varying opinions on different kinds of giving, and we do not want to go in that direction.

Jesus being our perfect example did not spend much time in His teaching talking about different types of giving. He focused on teaching the subject of giving. When we understand the subject of giving, we will not have to struggle in understanding the types of giving.

The concept of giving as a child of God is the transfer of valuable from one person to another to meet need as God directs, or as you're moved by God. This is to be considered the giving that comes from your heart - *as you purpose in your heart.* Giving this way delights God.

So let each one give as he purposes in his heart, not grudgingly or of necessity; for God loves a cheerful giver. 2 Corinthians 9:7.

As child of God, we're not supposed to give grudgingly or of necessity else we miss the reward from God. For such giving is not a response to God, but response to human pressure. Any form of giving could produce reward, but as a child of God, we are not interested in any kind of reward. We're interested in reward from God with eternal value.

And the reward from God does not just come by the act of giving alone, but by obeying **the instructions** that accompany the act of giving.

Weightier matters

If you pay tithe for instance, but neglect the weightier matters: justice, and mercy and faith, of what benefit? That's hypocrisy instead. Right?

*Woe to you, scribes and Pharisees, hypocrites! For you pay tithe of mint and anise and cummin, and have neglected the **weightier matters** of the law: justice and mercy and faith. These you ought to have done, without leaving the others undone. Matthew 23:23.*

To avoid hypocrisy as you pay tithe, do not neglect other matters that God considers weightier. You find it difficult to show mercy to your neighbor, yet you pay tithe. You struggle with matters of faith yet hold tithe so high. How well do you handle the issue of justice at your home, place of work, with your friends, and your kinsmen?

We see that the true tithe payers are not just those who pay ten percent of their income, it goes beyond that as the Lord points out. The list of record of tithe payers that some churches keep, must be weighed closely with the list that God has in heaven. In other words, we must allow God to hold the true list of the tithe payers and avoid confusing ourselves with list that might be filled with hypocrites! God is the rewarder, and He has the true list.

The size of your offering/contribution matters
The size of your offering is not measured with respect to other people's offering, but with respect to your earnings. One person could give hundred thousand naira as offering, while another gives two hundred thousand naira, yet the one who gave one hundred thousand naira has more value in measurement before God.

A relatively poor person with one hundred-thousand-naira offering has given more contribution than a millionaire who gave two hundred thousand naira in the same occasion.

Now Jesus sat opposite the treasury and saw how the people put money into the treasury. And many who were rich put in much. Then one poor widow came and threw in two mites, which make a quadrans. So He called His disciples to Himself and said to them, "Assuredly, I say to you that this poor widow has put in more than all those who have given to the treasury; for they all put in out of their abundance, but she out of her poverty put in all that she had, her whole livelihood." Mark 12:41-44.

We see from the text about, the contribution from the rich people and the contribution from the poor widow were both acceptable, but relatively, their measures before God were different. In spiritual scale, the poor widow gave more and will receive more reward. Her measure of reward will be higher than that of those rich people. For those rich people to be commended by the Lord as well, they'll have to give much more – they need to quit giving sparingly with respect to their earnings.

But this I say: He who sows sparingly will also reap sparingly, and he who sows bountifully will also reap bountifully. 2 Corinthians 9:6.

*Give, and it will be given to you: good measure, pressed down, shaken together, and running over will be put into your bosom. For with the **same measure** that you use, it will be measured back to you." Luke 6:38.*

Be in right standing with God
There are other cases where it is not just about the measure of the offering, but that both the person and the offering have problem before God. We see this in the life of Cain and Abel. Abel and his offering were respected by God, but Cain and his offering were not respected. It is not just the offering of Abel that was respected, but Abel and his offering. And it was not the offering of Cain that was not respected, but Cain and his offering. It is not just a question of whether the offering was big or small compared to their earnings, but that their lives also need to comply with God.

And in the process of time it came to pass that Cain brought an offering of the fruit of the ground to the Lord.

*Abel also brought of the firstborn of his flock and of their fat. And the Lord **respected Abel and his offering**, but **He did not respect Cain and his offering**. Genesis 4:3-5*

What offering will a harlot, liar, gossip, armed robber, murderer, backslider give to God that will make it acceptable. There is a need first for repentance.

So, we see again that not everyone who lines up to give offering to God is his or her offering acceptable to God. Can this explain why Jesus did not have to take offering from everyone that attends his services/crusade? Only certain brethren supported Jesus with substance during His ministry life.

And certain women who had been healed of evil spirits and infirmities —
Mary called Magdalene, out of whom had come seven demons, and Joanna the wife of Chuza, Herod's steward, and Susanna, and many others who provided for Him from their substance. Luke 8:2-3.

The Lord Jesus also told the parable of a brother who will have to leave his gift on the alter and go resolve problems with his brother first before having to come back to the altar to present the gift (Matthew 5: 23-24). We have to be right with God before our offering can be acceptable to Him. He's interested in us before our gift.

Giving alms
Let's look closely at the instruction from the Lord on giving alms to the needy. There are 3 parties involved in giving alms to the needy as instructed by God, namely:
- The giver
- The receiver, and
- Your Father in heaven

We cannot take God out of the equation in any form of giving. In giving alms, it is not just about the giver or the receiver but for the glory and praise of the Father.

"But to do good and to communicate forget not: for with such sacrifices God is well pleased". Hebrews 13:16.

To communicate in the text above is to distribute and contribute to the needy.

Giving alms to the needy as instructed by God does not require a show as some are inclined to do. They do so for their own self-love, interests, esteem, and ambition. They do it to be applauded and acknowledged by men. Give inconspicuously and the Lord will reward you openly and abundantly.

"*So **when you give** something to a needy person, **do not make a big show of it, as the hypocrites do in the houses of worship and on the streets**. They do it so that people will praise them. I assure you, they have already been **paid in full**. But when you help a needy person, do it in such a way that even your closest friend will not know about it. Then it will be a private matter. And your Father, who sees what you do in private, will reward you (Matthew 6:2-4 GNT).*

The devil will always present the applause and adulation of men as something good and extremely desirable, hence taking the focus off God and ultimately robbing you of your reward from the Father.

Act of worship

Giving alms the right way is never in vain. Your alms are a memorial before the Father. The story is told of Cornelius of whom the bible says *his prayers and his alms were come up for a memorial before God. Acts 10:4.*

His charitable actions which were from a principle of love and godly sincerity, were like sacrifices upon the altar which ascended to God with acceptance. Your giving of alms is always on record in heaven, in the book of remembrance and shall be remembered to your advantage and promotion.

We first offer ourselves to the Lord before our giving is acceptable to Him. So, giving is an act of worship.

The instruction from the command of giving to the needy starts with the phrase "when you give," it does not say "if you give." It is noteworthy that giving alms is not optional. God expects it, therefore settle it in your heart to give. Giving is of the heart and not a function of your pocket size or account balance. When you see someone in need, your heart is meant to be moved with compassion to meet their need. Be God's outstretched arms of love to all those around you.

It could be an instant decision
Giving can be either mandated or spontaneous.
A rich young man met Jesus and was asked to sell what he had and give the money to the poor and then follow Jesus. He never planned for such instructions, yet it was the very thing needed in his life for a turnaround.

Be generous
Dear friend, God is love. He demonstrated His love by giving us His best: His only begotten Son. Likewise, we ought to demonstrate our love for the Father in our giving. Remember it is more blessed to give than receive.

If you want to live in prosperity. Give. You cannot pray prosperity in. There are principles on prosperity. The bible says give and it shall be given unto you. Your prosperity is a function of your liberal soul (2 Corinthians 9:6-11).

The generous soul will be made rich, and he who waters will also be watered himself. Proverbs 11:25.

So dear child of God, to summarize this segment on giving, I will leave you with this, whatever the giving,

"Let each one (give) as he has made up his own mind and purposed in his heart, not reluctantly or sorrowfully or under compulsion, For God loves (He takes pleasure in, prizes above other things, and is unwilling to abandon or to do without) a cheerful (joyous, "prompt to do it") giver (whose heart is in his giving).

Simple instructions on prayer
And He spake a parable unto them to this end, that men ought always to pray, and not to faint. Luke 18:1

In the Amplified version, the word faint has been expanded to mean "not to turn coward, lose heart and give up.

Prayer is an integral part of the Christian walk, war, and work. Prayer is our fellowship, our communication with the Lord. Prayer cannot be replaced, neglected, or substituted with another activity. No matter how sincere and effective your giving is, it can never take the place of prayer. We must recognize prayer as a privilege as well as an honor.

Jesus was present with the disciples. They travelled with Him wherever He went. They witnessed all the miracles, participated in the meetings with the crowd. They were sent out and given power to perform miracles and cast out demons. Yet Jesus instructed them to watch and pray lest they fell into temptation. All the spiritual activities that they participated in could not take the place of prayer.

Note that the disciples of Jesus were Jews, and they knew how to pray religiously. After walking with Jesus for a while, they realized that Jesus didn't pray as they did. He actually had results continually in a way that startled and amazed them. They finally said to the Master *"Teach us to pray"*.

When we pray, we make tremendous power available, dynamic in its working, causing changes in our favour. Through prayer and in the Name of Jesus, we can change circumstances and alter destinies. What a blessing!

*"**When you pray**, do not be like the hypocrites! They love to stand up and pray in the houses of worship and on the street corners, **so that everyone will see them**. I assure you, they have already been paid in full.* **6 But when you pray, go to your room, close the door, and pray to your Father, who is unseen.** *And your Father, who sees what you do in private, will reward you. (Matthew 6:5-6 GNT)*

I said earlier that nothing can substitute prayer in the Christian faith.

There are those who live very active Christian lives. They are very diligent in their service, in attendance of services and all meetings including prayer meetings, evangelism etc. but have little or no personal time for prayer.

Martha, the sister of Mary found herself in a similar situation. The bible records that she was overly occupied and too busy and was distracted with much serving. Question? Who was she serving? It was Jesus. The Master had no issues with the service in itself but it had become a distraction to her. Her sister on the other hand, sat at Jesus' feet, in fellowship.

You must develop your personal prayer life. Practice being alone with God. The bible is replete with occasions when Jesus withdrew to be alone and pray.

On such one occasion, He sent the multitude away (and constrained His disciples to get into a ship and leave Him). *"When He had sent the multitudes away, He went up into a mountain apart to pray; and when the evening was come, he was there alone" Matthew 14:22-23*

The Master did not wait for a convenient time, He created the time. He did not wait for the people to leave in their own time, he sent them away. Dear child of God, learn to send people away, learn to put activities aside. Prioritize prayer. Things will always clamor for your attention: family, business, responsibilities, challenges. But you must learn to prioritize your time. Learn to isolate yourself. **Isolation comes before revelation.**

Like Jesus, you must understand the value and power of privacy with God.

*Matt 14:23 And when He had sent the multitudes away, He went up on the mountain **by Himself to pray**. Now when evening came, He was alone there. NKJV*

Now that you have succeeded in isolating yourself, what do you do in the time and place of prayer? Do you use the time to catalogue all your challenges, murmur, cry and complain?

I remember when I got my sales job. It was my first time directly engaged in sales, and I found it challenging meeting the set goals and targets. Of course, I decided I was going to pray about the job but without realizing it, I was just complaining before God and thought that was prayer. In one of such times, the Lord said to me "Get up and sit down. What you are doing is not prayer. You're complaining in the name of prayer. And that will not help you." I sat down as instructed and the

Lord began to furnish me with strategies to succeed on the job. As I applied these strategies, I not only did well in my sales target, but I was also given a raise, bonuses and an award. I was also promoted twice in two years; a first in the company's history.

Dear child of God, there is so much to share on prayer. If you must get the right results, learn to pray effectively: worship the Lord, give Him the honor due His Name and give Him thanks for all He has done. Search the scriptures to understand the mind of God concerning a matter and pray accordingly. Have faith when you pray, and nothing shall be impossible with you. Lastly always expect answers to your prayers.

"And this is the confidence (the assurance, the privilege of boldness) which we have in Him: (we are sure) that if we ask anything (make any request) according to His will (in agreement with His own plan), He listens to and hears us. And if (since) we (positively) know that He listens to us in whatsoever we ask, we also know (with settled and absolute knowledge) that we have granted us as our present possessions) the requests made of Him 1 John 5:13-14

An effective prayer life is transformational. It brings the power of God to bear on all that concerns you. Do not stop praying. The bible enjoins us to pray without ceasing (1st Thessalonians 5:17). It also mandates us to forgive while we stand praying (Mark 11:2526). If you struggle at the place of prayer, you will struggle in your Christian life.

Address the problem
*"For verily I say unto, that whosoever **shall say to this mountain,** be thou removed, and be thou cast into the sea; and shall not doubt in his heart but shall believe that those things which he saith shall come to pass, he shall have whatsoever he saith". Mark 11:23*

From the text, we can see clearly that God does not expect us to talk about the mountain or tell Him what to do about the mountain. You are to address the mountain and tell it what to do. The content of your prayer must be directed towards the specific area of need, or you may not have the desired results. You must speak what you want to see, and God will make it happen by His power.

When Jesus woke up and saw the windstorm, He did not start by making the windstorm the subject of discussion, *He rebuked the wind, and said to the sea, "Peace, be still!" And the wind ceased and there was a great calm. Mark 4:39.*

Simple instructions on fasting
*"And **when you fast**, do not put on a sad face as the hypocrites do. They neglect their appearance so that everyone will see that they are fasting. I assure you, they have already been paid in full. 17 **When you go without food, wash your face and comb your hair, 18 so that others cannot know that you are fasting — only your Father, who is unseen, will know.** And your Father, who sees what you do in private, will reward you (Matthew 6:16-18 GNT)*

Fasting is all about conditioning your spirit to receive from God. It involves putting the body under subjection by abstaining from food, water or any other specific thing or activity to receive from God.

Is this not the fast that I have chosen: to loose the bonds of wickedness, to undo the heavy burdens, to let the oppressed go free, and that you break every yoke? Isaiah 58:6.

Jesus isolated Himself and fasted in preparation for His ministry. As with giving and prayer, fasting is not optional. Some local assembles may have corporate fasts which is great but as a Christian, you should have your own personal fasting time and schedule.

One of the things that helped me get back on my feet after 15 years of an unstable and unproductive Christian life was a schedule of consistent fasting. During those periods, my appetite for, and understanding of God's word grew larger and deeper. That lifestyle of continual fasting made a humongous difference in my life and it has been from strength to strength and from glory to glory ever since.

Be wise:
*Another parable spake he unto them; The kingdom of heaven is like unto leaven, which a woman took, and **hid in three measures of meal**, till the whole was leavened. Matt 13:33 KJV*

Do you have secrets?
Do you keep secrets?
The bible talks about the secret things belonging to the Lord. (Deuteronomy 29:29). With God there are some things that are kept secret. He doesn't reveal or divulge everything.

Dear friend, do you know that there are things that God is doing with or in you that He does not want disclosed. Many a time, things that began so beautifully never come to fruition because of a premature disclosure.

We know the story of Samson, if he kept the secret about his anointing, the enemy could not defeat him. Once he was lured into sharing his secret, he was robbed of God's power and glory. He also paid for that mistake with his life.

And how I kept back nothing that was profitable unto you, but have shewed you, and have taught you publickly, and from house to house.
Acts 20:20.

Paul said he kept back nothing that was profitable for their souls. He told the people everything he was commanded by God to tell them.

There are bits of information that are good but unprofitable to the hearer at the time. Some have excitedly and albeit prematurely, testified about God's work in their lives and cut short the process. I have heard sad stories of how young ladies in their excitement tell their friends or family about their budding plans to settle down, and once the news is leaked, the man in question suddenly develops cold feet and loses interest altogether. Dear child of God, learn to be discreet about events and happenings in your life. At the right time, the Lord will direct you accordingly.

And the temple, when it was being built, was built with stone finished at the quarry, **so that no hammer or chisel or any iron tool was heard in the temple while it was being built.** *1 Kings 6:7.*

The bible tells us that it is God at work in you both to will and to do of His good pleasure. Right now, you are work in progress. What are you building? –

spiritual life, contacts, relationships, business, marriage, family, career? The text above tells us no noise was heard while the temple was being built. Are you wise enough to be quiet and discreet or are you spreading the news of the ongoing work in your life? Let God guide you in every step. Love does not mean trust. Learn to build in silence. There will surely be a time when it will be okay to disclose the matter.

Dear child of God, learn to speak at the right time. Remember there are some things God is doing in your life that should be kept under wraps till the proper time of disclosure. Some information about your life may enrage even those you feel love you and are close to you and the enemy may turn them against you.

Even the mystery which hath been hid from ages and from generations, but now is made manifest to His saints. Colossians 1:26.

Even God Himself did not reveal the mystery of salvation in Christ to the patriarchs and prophets of old, even though they searched and enquired diligently. 1 Peter 1:10-12.

Very often, it is not demonic activities that stop the manifestation of God's power and glory in our lives and society but disobedience of the simplest of instructions; some as simple as "be quiet."

Conclusion
For our love for God means that we obey his commands. And his commands are not too hard for us, because every child of God is able to defeat the world. And we win the victory over the world by means of our faith. 1 John 5:3-4 GNT.

This Book of the Law shall not depart from your mouth, but you shall meditate in it day and night, that you may observe to do according to all that is written in it. For then you will make your way prosperous, and then you will have good success. Joshua 1:8.

The Lord said, "*come* unto me, all ye that labour and are heavy laden, and I will give you rest". (Matthew 11:28).

God expects us to come to him with our concerns, needs, challenges and burdens to receive His guidance and help. *He said, **come** let us reason together… (Isaiah 1:18-20).*

God is still beckoning on us to come to Him with that matter. He is the extraordinary strategist and has the capacity to bring about the change we need. For it is not by our might nor by our power but by the Spirit says the Lord (Zechariah 4:6).

In my personal life, I had struggled with addiction to pornography for instance and associated masturbation from my days in secondary school. I had overhead a classmate of mine discuss the act. I got fascinated and tried it out at home and got hooked. Thanks to God, I was freed from that bondage when I gave my life to Christ. After a while, due to lack of a thriving fellowship with God and insufficient knowledge of God's Word, I got overpowered by the temptation and went back to pornography. The addiction persisted for over a decade right into the early years of my marriage. In those days I compelled my wife to be an accomplice by sending her out to purchase the pornographic movies for our viewing pleasure. I reasoned that being married was God's endorsement to watch or do whatever I liked.

When I gave my attention to God's Word with the godly counsel of a dear brother, Bro Omeje Herbert, that satanic influence was permanently broken. Till today, I am still enjoying this liberty and my marriage is stable and flourishing.

Dear friend, there is no vacuum in life. Any empty space or unutilized time gets filled up with whatever that is available. If you leave your life, mind, time, schedules, priorities open and unguarded, the devil will sow destruction.

Your life is like a garden. When planted with good seed and adequately enclosed, will produce good fruit and be free of satanic intrusions.

Dear child of God, you cannot grow and flourish as a Christian without a robust and unbroken fellowship with the Spirit and the Word of God. When you give this the preeminence in life, you shall experience evident transformations daily in every area of your life. You shall live in absolute dominion over the circumstances of life, and please the Father in all things.

Arise, shine; for thy light is come, and the glory of the LORD is risen upon thee. Isaiah 60:1.

Printed in Great Britain
by Amazon